# Pet Cats

By Debbie Croft

A cat is a pet.

Ben has a pet cat.

His cat is Pep.

Ben

Pep

3

It is Pen.

Tips is her pet cat.

Pen can pat Tips.

Pat, pat, pat!

Ren has a pet cat.

His cat is Sim.

Sim can sit at a mat.

Sim sips!

Sim

*Sip, sip, sip!*

It is Bec and her pet cat.

Her cat is Tab.

Tab can hit and hit.

He is fit!

Bec

Tab

# CHECKING FOR MEANING

1. What is the name of Pen's cat? *(Literal)*

2. Which cat can sit at a mat to sip? *(Literal)*

3. What does Tab hit? *(Inferential)*

# EXTENDING VOCABULARY

| | |
|---|---|
| **can** | Find the small word at the end of *can*. Change the letter *c* to make other new words. |
| **pat** | Look at the word *pat*. Take out the *a* and put in *e*, *i* or *o*. What new words does this make? |
| **fit** | What are two different meanings of the word *fit*? In this text, what does it mean that Tab is fit? |

# MOVING BEYOND THE TEXT

1. Which words would you use to describe how it feels to pat a cat with your hand?

2. What makes a cat a good pet to own?

3. What do you need to do to take good care of a pet cat?

4. What are the names of some big cats that live in the wild?

## SPEED SOUNDS

| Cc | Bb | Rr | Ee | Ff | Hh | Nn |
|----|----|----|----|----|----|----|

| Mm | Ss | Aa | Pp | Ii | Tt |
|----|----|----|----|----|----|

# PRACTICE WORDS

pet

cat

Ben

Pep

Pen

Ren

Bec

fit

can

Tab

hit